MANDALAS

Adult Coloring Book

Kevin Hwu

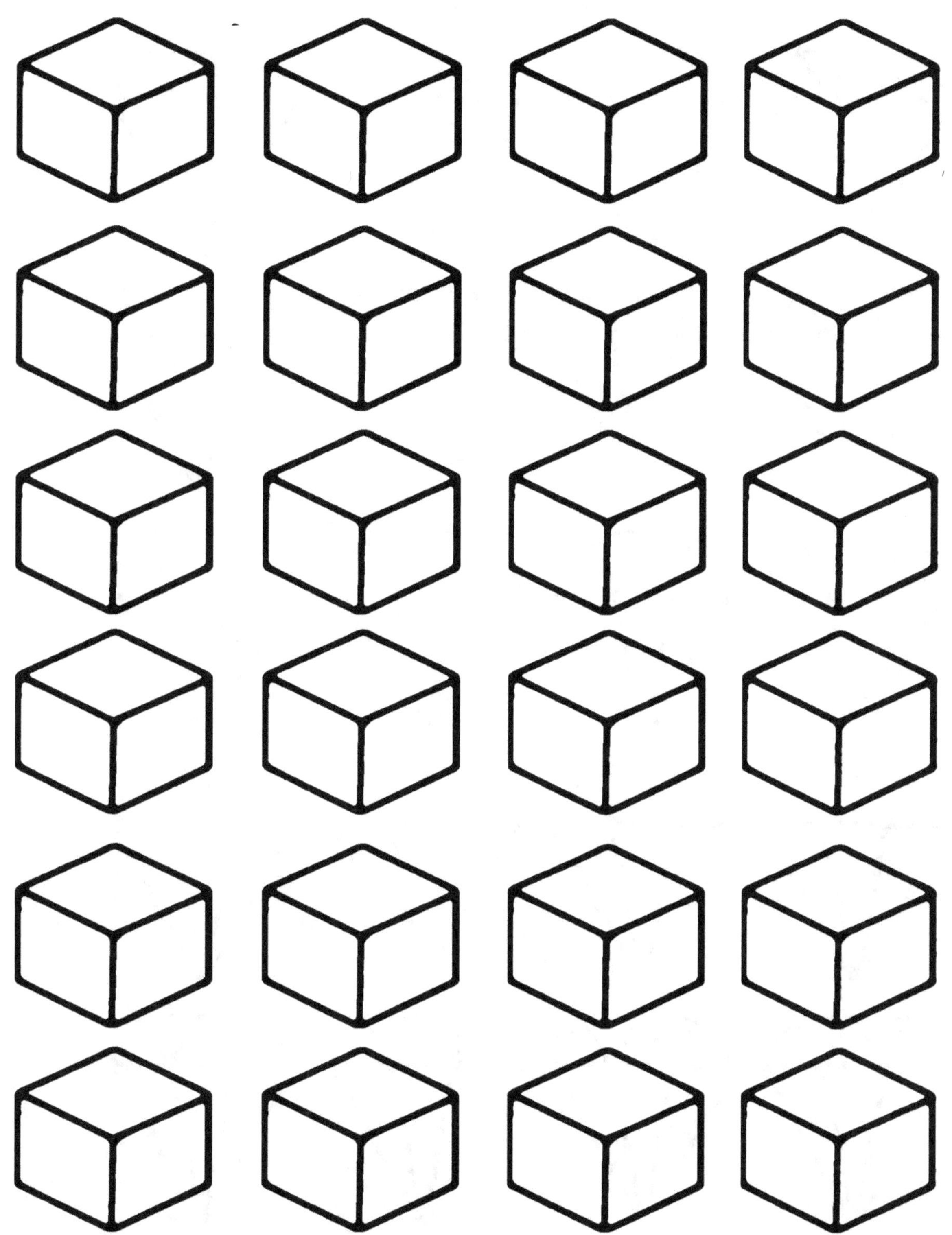

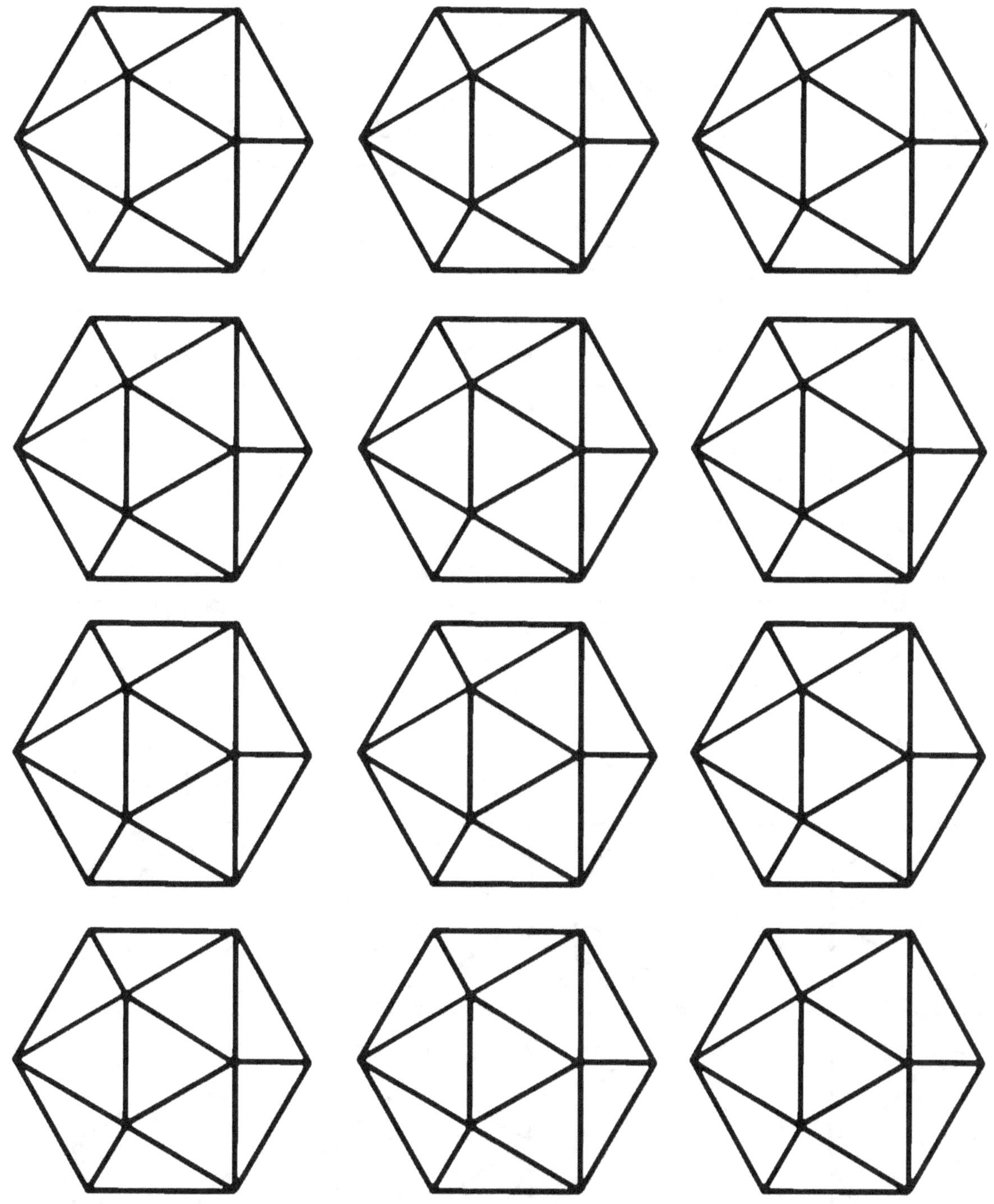

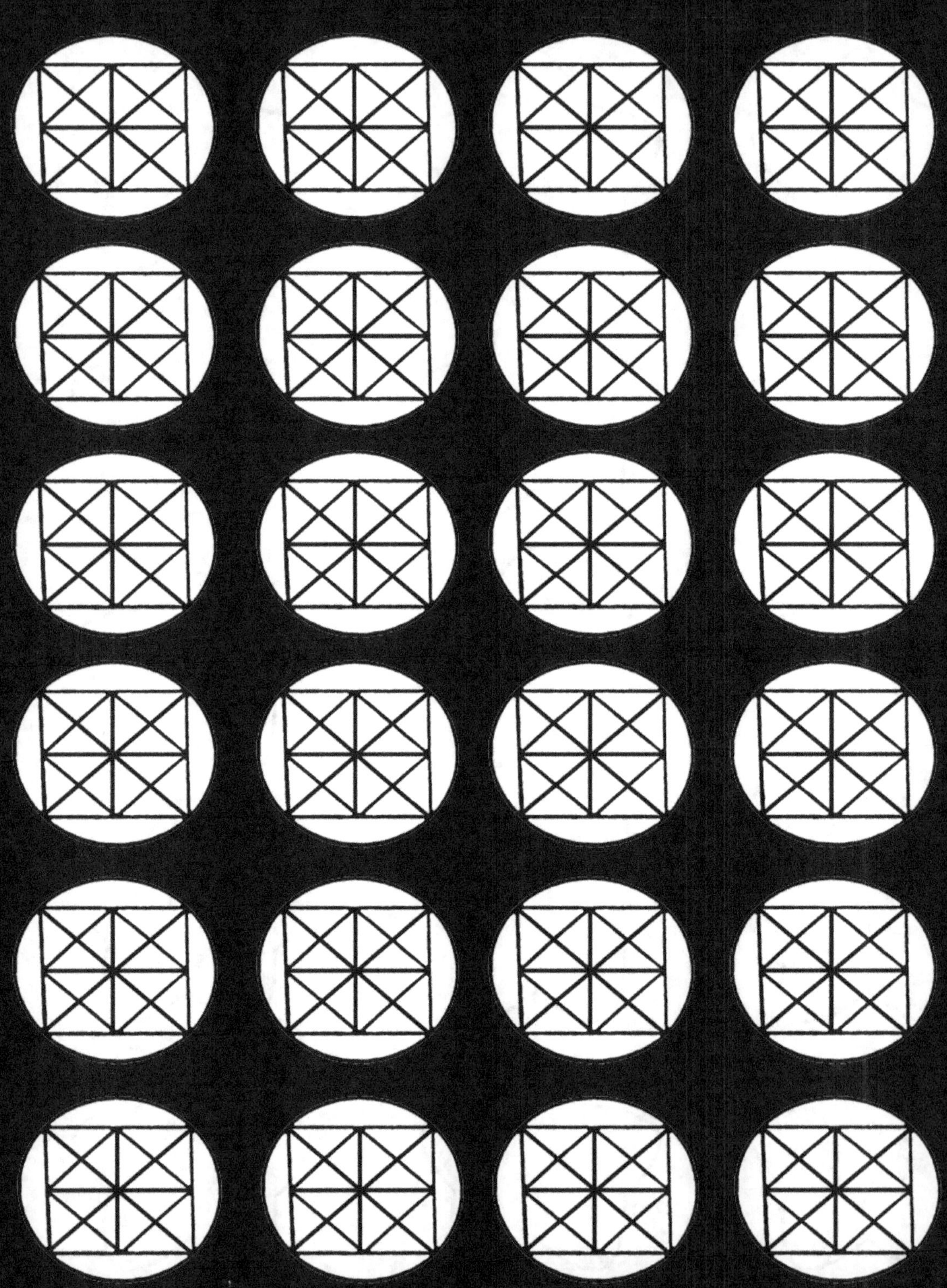

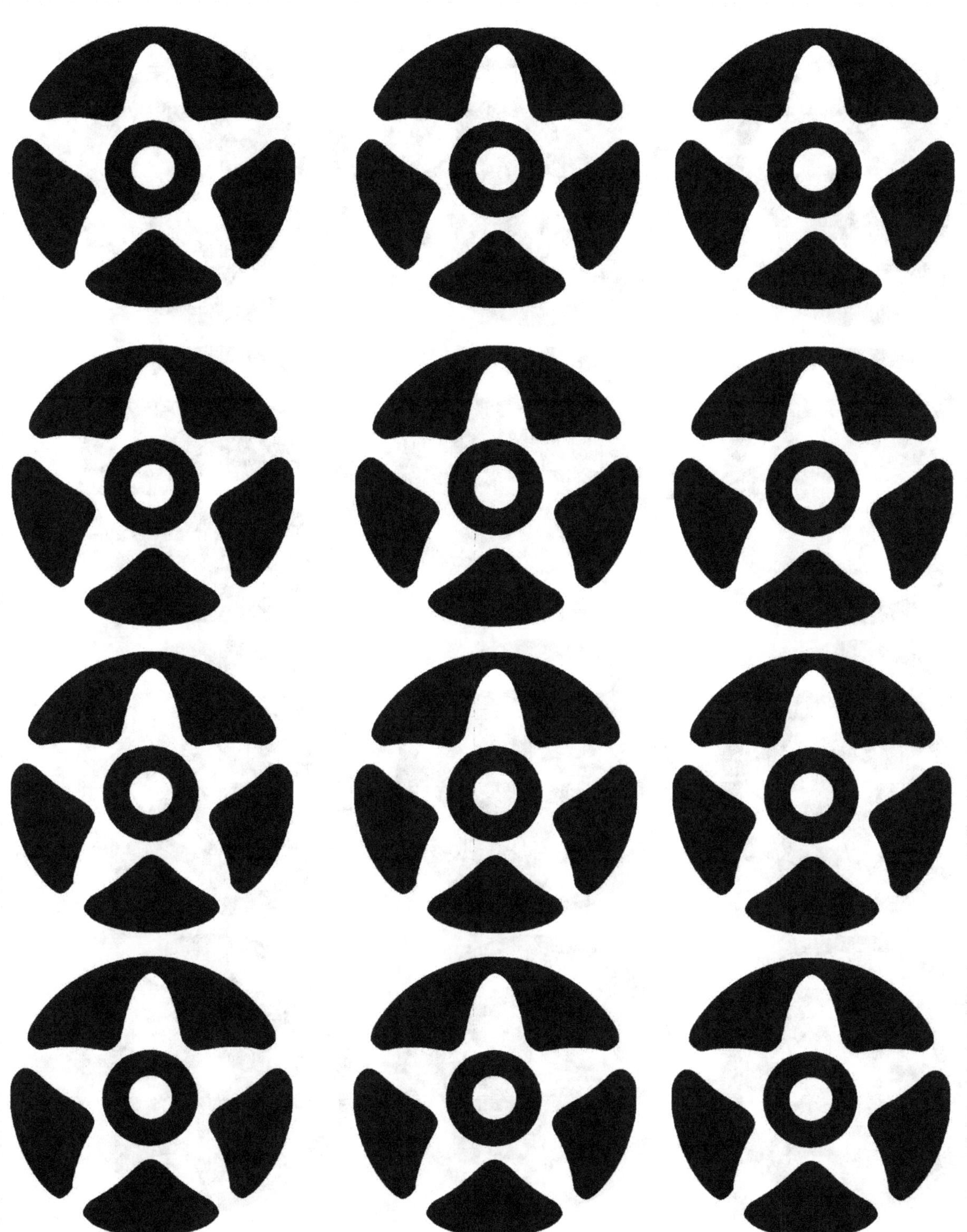

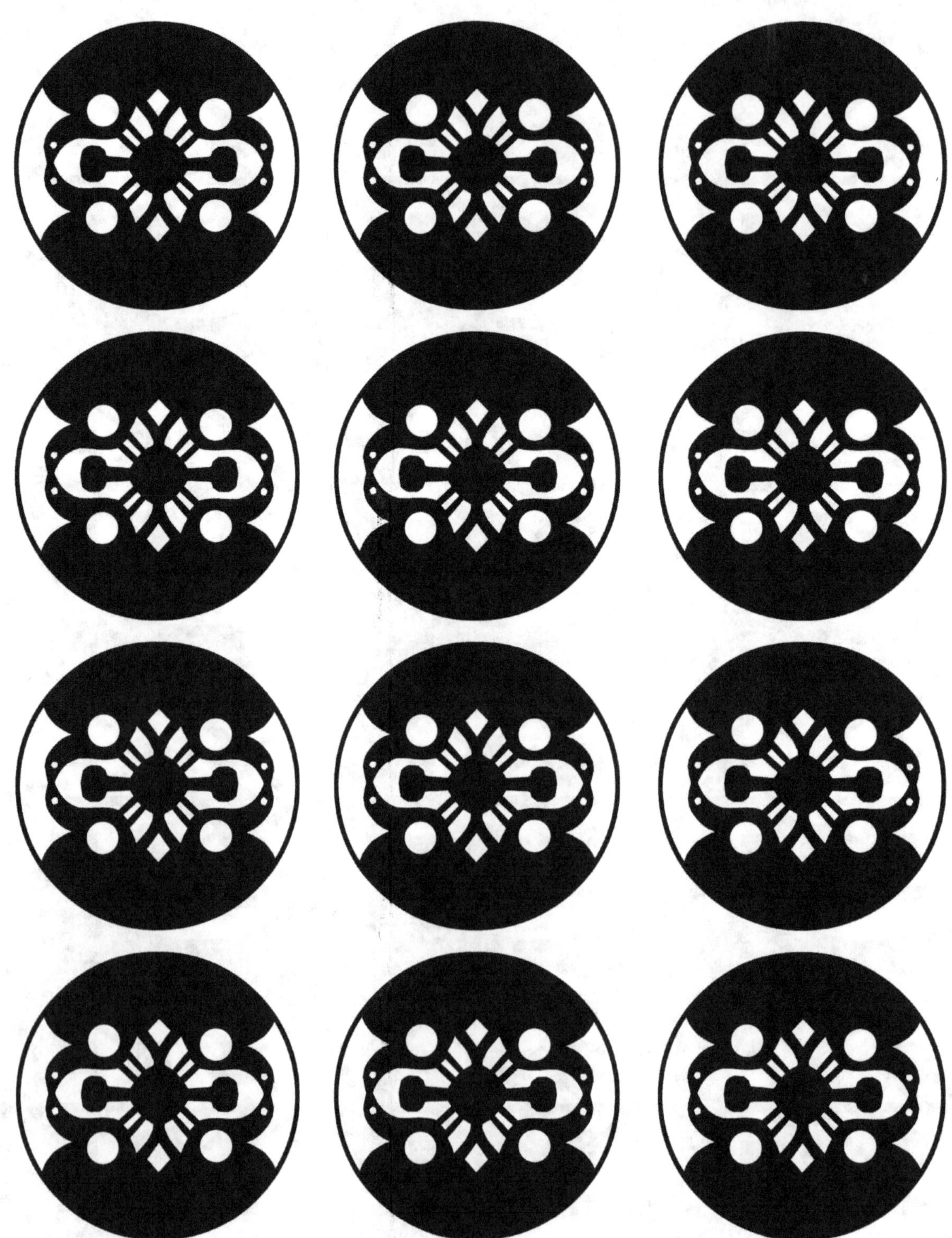

Copyright © 2017

All rights reserved.

No part of this publication may be copied, reproduced in any format, by any means, electronic or otherwise, without prior consent fromthe copyright owner and publisher of this book.

Disclaimer

The information contained in this ebook is for general informationpurposes only. The information is provided by the authors and while we endeavor to keep the information up to date and correct, we make no representations or warranties of any kind, express or implied, aboutthe completeness, accuracy, reliability, suitability or availability with respect to the ebook or the information, products, services, or relatedgraphics contained in the ebook for any purpose. Any reliance youplace on such information is therefore strictly at your own risk.